EMMANUEL JOSEPH

The Social Kitchen, How Culinary Traditions and Robotics Shape Modern Communities

Copyright © 2025 by Emmanuel Joseph

All rights reserved. No part of this publication may be reproduced, stored or transmitted in any form or by any means, electronic, mechanical, photocopying, recording, scanning, or otherwise without written permission from the publisher. It is illegal to copy this book, post it to a website, or distribute it by any other means without permission.

First edition

This book was professionally typeset on Reedsy. Find out more at reedsy.com

Contents

1	Chapter 1: The Heartbeat of the Home	1
2	Chapter 2: Culinary Traditions and Cultural Identity	3
3	Chapter 3: The Evolution of the Social Kitchen	5
4	Chapter 4: The Rise of Robotics in the Kitchen	7
5	Chapter 5: Enhancing Culinary Creativity with Technology	9
6	Chapter 6: The Impact of Robotics on Culinary Education	11
7	Chapter 7: Community-Building Through Food and Technology	13
8	Chapter 8: The Role of Robotics in Sustainable Cooking	15
9	Chapter 9: The Future of Smart Kitchens	17
10	Chapter 10: Bridging the Gap Between Home Cooks and...	19
11	Chapter 11: The Intersection of Culinary Traditions and...	21
12	Chapter 12: Embracing the Social Kitchen of Tomorrow	23
13	Chapter 13: Culinary Traditions in the Digital Age	24
14	Chapter 14: The Role of Robotics in Professional Kitchens	26
15	Chapter 15: The Influence of Food Bloggers and Influencers	28
16	Chapter 16: The Future of Home Cooking with Robotics	30
17	Chapter 17: The Social Impact of Culinary Innovation	32

1

Chapter 1: The Heartbeat of the Home

The kitchen has always been more than just a place to prepare meals; it's the beating heart of a home, where families gather, share stories, and create memories. Culinary traditions passed down through generations hold a wealth of cultural history and family lore, making each dish a tangible connection to the past. These traditions reflect the values and lifestyles of their times, from elaborate feasts to humble home-cooked meals. In an ever-changing world, the kitchen remains a constant, grounding families and communities in their shared heritage.

Mealtimes have always been central to family life, providing a structured time for connection amidst the hustle and bustle of daily routines. These moments around the table foster communication and unity, allowing family members to share their experiences and support one another. The rituals of setting the table, serving food, and enjoying a meal together create a sense of belonging and continuity that extends beyond the kitchen walls. The kitchen, therefore, is not merely a physical space but a repository of cherished memories and shared experiences.

As societies evolve and lifestyles change, the role of the kitchen adapts accordingly. In modern homes, the kitchen is often an open and inviting space designed for social interaction and collaboration. The integration of dining areas and living spaces blurs the boundaries between cooking and entertaining, making the kitchen a central hub for social gatherings. This evolution reflects the importance of the kitchen as a place where bonds are strengthened and community is built.

Moreover, the kitchen serves as a canvas for creativity and self-expression. Through cooking, individuals can experiment with flavors, textures, and techniques, transforming ingredients into dishes that tell a story. This creative process is deeply personal, allowing cooks to infuse their unique style and personality into their culinary creations. The kitchen, therefore, is not just a place to nourish the body but also a space to nourish the soul, fostering a sense of accomplishment and fulfillment.

2

Chapter 2: Culinary Traditions and Cultural Identity

C uisine plays a vital role in defining cultural identity, encapsulating the flavors, ingredients, and cooking methods unique to different regions. Traditional dishes are often tied to specific celebrations, rituals, and customs, reinforcing a sense of belonging and continuity. Whether it's the spices of Indian cuisine, the pasta of Italy, or the street food of Nigeria, each culinary tradition tells a story about the people and places from which it originates. As communities migrate and blend, these traditions evolve, but their core essence remains a powerful link to one's roots.

Food is a universal language that transcends borders and unites people across cultures. Sharing a meal is an act of hospitality and generosity, fostering connections and breaking down barriers. In multicultural societies, culinary traditions from different parts of the world come together, creating a vibrant tapestry of flavors and influences. This blending of cuisines reflects the dynamic nature of cultural identity, which is continually shaped by the exchange of ideas and experiences.

The preservation of culinary traditions is essential for maintaining cultural heritage and passing it on to future generations. Family recipes, handed down through the years, carry with them the wisdom and experiences of those who came before. These recipes are more than just instructions for preparing a dish; they are a means of storytelling, preserving the history and values of a community. By keeping these traditions alive, we honor our ancestors and ensure that their legacy endures.

As we navigate the complexities of modern life, culinary traditions offer a sense of stability and comfort. In times of change and uncertainty, familiar flavors and aromas can evoke memories of home and provide a sense of reassurance. The act of cooking and sharing a traditional meal can strengthen family bonds and create a sense of continuity, anchoring us in our cultural identity and providing a sense of belonging.

3

Chapter 3: The Evolution of the Social Kitchen

The concept of the kitchen has evolved over time, influenced by technological advancements and societal changes. From open hearths to modern smart kitchens, the way we cook and interact within this space has transformed dramatically. Today's kitchens are not only functional spaces but also social hubs equipped with the latest gadgets and appliances. These innovations have changed the dynamics of meal preparation, allowing for more collaboration and interaction among family members and guests. The social kitchen continues to adapt, reflecting the changing needs and lifestyles of contemporary society.

In the past, the kitchen was often a separate and utilitarian space, hidden away from the main living areas. Cooking was seen as a solitary task, primarily performed by women, with little involvement from other family members. However, as societal norms shifted and the roles within the household evolved, the kitchen became a more inclusive and interactive space. The rise of open-plan living, where the kitchen is integrated with the dining and living areas, has transformed it into a focal point for social gatherings and family activities.

Technological advancements have played a significant role in shaping the modern kitchen. The introduction of labor-saving appliances, such as dishwashers, microwaves, and food processors, has made cooking more efficient and less time-consuming. Smart kitchen technology, including connected appliances, voice-activated assistants, and automated systems, is further revolutionizing the way we cook and interact in the kitchen. These innovations not only enhance convenience but also create opportunities for creativity and experimentation.

The social kitchen of today is a space where people come together to cook, eat, and connect. It is a place for collaboration, where family members and friends can share in the joy of preparing and enjoying a meal. Cooking has become a shared activity, fostering communication and strengthening relationships. The kitchen is no longer just a place to prepare food; it is a vibrant and dynamic environment that reflects the social and cultural values of contemporary society.

4

Chapter 4: The Rise of Robotics in the Kitchen

With the advent of robotics, the kitchen is undergoing yet another revolution. Robots and AI-powered devices are becoming increasingly common, assisting with tasks such as chopping, cooking, and cleaning. These advancements are not only making meal preparation more efficient but also opening up new possibilities for culinary creativity. Robotic technology is helping to bridge the gap between professional chefs and home cooks, making gourmet cooking accessible to a wider audience. As robots become more integrated into our daily lives, they are transforming the way we approach food and cooking.

Robotic kitchen assistants, such as automated cooking systems and robotic arms, can perform precise and repetitive tasks with a high degree of accuracy. These devices can handle a wide range of cooking techniques, from sautéing and grilling to baking and steaming. By taking over routine tasks, robots free up time for cooks to focus on more complex and creative aspects of meal preparation. This increased efficiency can lead to a more enjoyable and rewarding cooking experience.

In addition to assisting with meal preparation, robotics is also playing a role in enhancing food safety and hygiene. Automated systems can monitor and control cooking temperatures, reducing the risk of foodborne illnesses.

Robotic cleaners can maintain a spotless kitchen environment, ensuring that surfaces and utensils are free from contaminants. These innovations contribute to a safer and healthier kitchen, benefiting both home cooks and professional chefs.

The integration of robotics into the kitchen is also fostering greater inclusivity. For individuals with physical disabilities or limitations, robotic devices can provide valuable assistance, enabling them to participate in cooking activities that might otherwise be challenging. By making the kitchen more accessible, robotics is empowering people of all abilities to enjoy the pleasures of cooking and dining.

5

Chapter 5: Enhancing Culinary Creativity with Technology

Technology is enabling new levels of culinary creativity, allowing chefs and home cooks to experiment with flavors, textures, and presentation in ways that were previously unimaginable. From 3D food printing to molecular gastronomy, innovative tools and techniques are pushing the boundaries of traditional cooking. Robotics and AI are also playing a role in this creative revolution, offering precise control and consistency that can elevate dishes to new heights. As technology continues to advance, the possibilities for culinary innovation are limitless, inspiring a new generation of chefs and food enthusiasts.

3D food printing is one of the most exciting developments in modern gastronomy, allowing chefs to create intricate and visually stunning dishes with unparalleled precision. This technology enables the layering of different ingredients to form complex shapes and designs, transforming food into edible art. The ability to customize and personalize dishes opens up new avenues for creativity, allowing chefs to experiment with novel combinations of flavors and textures.

Molecular gastronomy, another frontier of culinary innovation, uses scientific principles to manipulate ingredients and create unique dining experiences. Techniques such as spherification, foaming, and gelification allow chefs to deconstruct and reimagine traditional dishes, challenging diners' perceptions and expectations. Robotics and AI play a crucial role in this process, providing the precision and control needed to execute these techniques flawlessly.

AI-powered tools and devices are also enhancing the culinary creativity of home cooks. Smart ovens, for example, can adjust cooking times and temperatures based on the type of food being prepared, ensuring perfect results every time. Recipe recommendation algorithms can suggest personalized meal ideas based on individual preferences and dietary restrictions, encouraging cooks to try new ingredients and techniques. These innovations are democratizing culinary creativity, making it accessible to a broader audience.

The fusion of technology and culinary art is fostering a collaborative and experimental spirit within the culinary community. Chefs, scientists, and technologists are working together to explore new possibilities and push the boundaries of what is possible in the kitchen. This interdisciplinary approach is driving innovation and inspiring a new generation of culinary pioneers, who are redefining the art of cooking and creating unforgettable dining experiences.

6

Chapter 6: The Impact of Robotics on Culinary Education

Robotics is not only changing the way we cook but also how we learn about cooking. Culinary schools and training programs are incorporating robotic technology into their curricula, providing students with hands-on experience with the latest tools and techniques. This integration is helping to prepare the next generation of chefs for a future where technology plays a central role in the kitchen. By embracing robotics, culinary education is evolving to meet the demands of a rapidly changing industry, ensuring that students are equipped with the skills and knowledge needed to succeed in a tech-driven world.

Incorporating robotics into culinary education offers several benefits. Students can learn to operate and program robotic kitchen assistants, gaining practical experience with the tools that will shape the future of cooking. These skills are becoming increasingly valuable as the industry moves towards greater automation and digitization. By familiarizing students with cutting-edge technology, culinary schools are equipping them with a competitive edge in the job market.

Robotics also enhances the learning experience by providing opportunities for experimentation and innovation. Students can use AI-powered devices to test new recipes, adjust cooking parameters, and analyze the results in real-time. This hands-on approach fosters a deeper understanding of the principles of cooking and encourages creative problem-solving. By integrating robotics into their training, students can develop the confidence and expertise needed to excel in a rapidly evolving culinary landscape.

The use of robotics in culinary education is also promoting inclusivity and accessibility. Robotic devices can assist students with physical disabilities, enabling them to participate fully in cooking activities. By making the kitchen more inclusive, culinary schools are fostering a diverse and supportive learning environment, where all students can thrive. This commitment to inclusivity is essential for nurturing the next generation of culinary talent and ensuring that the industry reflects the diversity of the communities it serves.

As the culinary world continues to embrace technology, the role of robotics in education will only grow. By staying at the forefront of innovation, culinary schools can ensure that their graduates are well-prepared for the challenges and opportunities of the future. The integration of robotics into culinary education is not just about teaching technical skills; it's about inspiring a new generation of chefs to push the boundaries of what is possible in the kitchen and to reimagine the art of cooking.

7

Chapter 7: Community-Building Through Food and Technology

Food has always been a powerful tool for building community, bringing people together around a shared table. With the help of technology, this sense of community is being amplified, connecting individuals and groups in new and meaningful ways. Online platforms and social media are allowing people to share recipes, cooking tips, and culinary experiences with a global audience. Virtual cooking classes and live-streamed food events are creating opportunities for engagement and collaboration, fostering a sense of unity and belonging. As technology continues to evolve, it will play an increasingly important role in strengthening social bonds through food.

Social media platforms like Instagram, YouTube, and TikTok have become vibrant spaces for culinary creativity and community-building. Home cooks and professional chefs alike share their culinary journeys, showcasing their recipes, techniques, and kitchen adventures. These platforms provide a space for interaction and feedback, allowing individuals to connect over their shared love of food. The accessibility of these platforms means that anyone, regardless of their location or background, can participate and contribute to the global culinary conversation.

Virtual cooking classes and live-streamed food events have emerged as popular ways to engage with the culinary community. These online gatherings allow participants to learn from expert chefs, exchange ideas, and share their culinary creations in real-time. The interactive nature of these events fosters a sense of camaraderie and connection, bringing people together in a virtual space to celebrate the joys of cooking and eating. This virtual engagement is particularly valuable in times of social distancing, providing a way for individuals to stay connected and engaged with their culinary passions.

Technology is also enabling new forms of culinary collaboration and innovation. Crowdsourced recipe platforms and cooking apps allow users to contribute their own recipes, rate and review others, and collaborate on new culinary projects. These platforms create a dynamic and interactive culinary ecosystem, where ideas and inspiration can be shared and refined collectively. The collaborative nature of these platforms fosters a sense of community and creativity, encouraging individuals to explore new culinary horizons and push the boundaries of their cooking skills.

As technology continues to shape the culinary landscape, it will play an increasingly important role in building and strengthening community. By providing new ways for people to connect, share, and collaborate, technology is enhancing the social aspects of cooking and dining. The social kitchen of the future will be a place where technology and tradition intersect, creating a dynamic and inclusive space for culinary exploration and community-building.

8

Chapter 8: The Role of Robotics in Sustainable Cooking

Sustainability is a growing concern in the culinary world, and robotics is helping to address some of the challenges associated with sustainable cooking. From reducing food waste to optimizing energy use, robotic technology is making it easier to adopt eco-friendly practices in the kitchen. Automated systems can monitor and manage resources more efficiently, minimizing waste and reducing the environmental impact of cooking. By incorporating robotics into sustainable cooking practices, we can create a more environmentally conscious approach to food preparation, benefiting both people and the planet.

One of the key ways robotics can contribute to sustainability is through the reduction of food waste. Intelligent systems can track expiration dates, monitor inventory levels, and suggest recipes based on available ingredients, ensuring that food is used before it goes to waste. These systems can also help with portion control, minimizing excess and reducing the amount of food that is discarded. By leveraging technology to manage food resources more effectively, we can make significant strides toward reducing waste and promoting sustainability in the kitchen.

Energy efficiency is another area where robotics can make a positive impact. Smart appliances and automated systems can optimize energy use, adjusting cooking times and temperatures based on the specific needs of each dish. For example, an AI-powered oven can preheat only when necessary and maintain precise temperature control, reducing energy consumption. These technologies not only save energy but also enhance the overall efficiency of the cooking process, making it more environmentally friendly.

Robotics also has the potential to revolutionize urban farming and food production. Automated systems can manage indoor and vertical farms, optimizing water and nutrient use and maximizing crop yields. By bringing food production closer to urban centers, these innovations can reduce the carbon footprint associated with transporting food over long distances. This approach not only supports sustainable agriculture but also ensures that fresh, locally grown produce is readily available to consumers.

The integration of robotics into sustainable cooking practices is a promising development that aligns with the broader goals of environmental stewardship and resource conservation. By embracing these technologies, we can create a more sustainable and resilient food system, one that meets the needs of the present without compromising the ability of future generations to meet their own needs.

9

Chapter 9: The Future of Smart Kitchens

The smart kitchen of the future is a seamless blend of tradition and technology, where culinary heritage meets cutting-edge innovation. Equipped with AI-powered appliances, voice-activated assistants, and connected devices, these kitchens are designed to enhance the cooking experience while maintaining a focus on convenience and efficiency. The integration of robotics and smart technology is creating a new era of culinary possibilities, where personalized meal plans, automated cooking, and intelligent kitchen management are becoming the norm. As these technologies continue to develop, the future of the kitchen promises to be an exciting and dynamic space.

Smart kitchens are equipped with a range of connected devices that communicate with each other to streamline the cooking process. For example, a smart refrigerator can keep track of inventory, suggest recipes based on available ingredients, and even place orders for groceries when supplies run low. Voice-activated assistants can provide step-by-step cooking instructions, adjust cooking settings, and answer questions in real-time, making it easier for cooks to multitask and stay organized.

Automated cooking systems are another hallmark of the smart kitchen. These devices can prepare entire meals with minimal human intervention, using precise measurements and cooking techniques to achieve consistent results. For example, a smart oven can preheat itself, adjust cooking times and temperatures, and notify the cook when the meal is ready. This level of automation not only saves time but also ensures that dishes are cooked to perfection every time.

Personalization is a key feature of the smart kitchen, with AI-powered systems tailoring meal plans and cooking recommendations to individual preferences and dietary needs. These systems can learn from user behavior, tracking likes and dislikes, and suggesting new recipes to try. By offering personalized guidance and support, smart kitchens make it easier for individuals to maintain a healthy and enjoyable diet.

The future of smart kitchens also includes advancements in kitchen design and layout. Modular and flexible designs allow for customization and adaptability, accommodating a wide range of cooking styles and preferences. Smart countertops and surfaces can provide interactive displays, offering cooking tips, nutritional information, and entertainment options while preparing meals. These innovations create a more immersive and engaging cooking experience, blending functionality with aesthetic appeal.

10

Chapter 10: Bridging the Gap Between Home Cooks and Professional Chefs

Robotics is helping to bridge the gap between home cooks and professional chefs, making advanced cooking techniques more accessible to everyone. With the assistance of AI-powered devices and robotic tools, home cooks can achieve restaurant-quality results with ease. These technologies are democratizing the culinary world, allowing people of all skill levels to explore their passion for cooking and experiment with new recipes. By leveling the playing field, robotics is fostering a greater appreciation for the art of cooking and inspiring a new generation of food enthusiasts.

One of the most significant ways robotics is bridging the gap is through precision and consistency. Professional chefs rely on precise measurements and techniques to create dishes of the highest quality. Robotic kitchen assistants can replicate these techniques with incredible accuracy, ensuring that home cooks can achieve the same level of precision in their own kitchens. For example, a robotic sous-chef can handle delicate tasks such as chopping, mixing, and plating, allowing home cooks to focus on other aspects of the meal.

AI-powered cooking systems also provide home cooks with expert guidance and support. These systems can offer step-by-step instructions, suggest adjustments based on user feedback, and even troubleshoot issues in real-time. This level of assistance empowers home cooks to tackle complex recipes and techniques with confidence, expanding their culinary repertoire and enhancing their skills. The ability to receive personalized feedback and recommendations from AI systems further accelerates the learning process, helping home cooks to continuously improve.

The availability of advanced cooking technology is making it easier for home cooks to experiment with new ingredients and techniques. Devices such as precision cookers, sous-vide machines, and 3D food printers are becoming more affordable and accessible, allowing home cooks to explore the cutting-edge of culinary innovation. These tools open up new possibilities for creativity and experimentation, enabling home cooks to push the boundaries of traditional cooking and discover new flavors and textures.

By making advanced cooking techniques more accessible, robotics is fostering a greater appreciation for the culinary arts. Home cooks are gaining a deeper understanding of the principles and processes that underpin professional cooking, leading to a more informed and engaged culinary community. This democratization of culinary knowledge is inspiring a new generation of food enthusiasts, who are passionate about exploring the art of cooking and sharing their creations with others.

11

Chapter 11: The Intersection of Culinary Traditions and Modern Technology

The intersection of culinary traditions and modern technology is creating a rich tapestry of flavors, techniques, and experiences. By embracing both the old and the new, we can honor our culinary heritage while exploring the possibilities of the future. Robotics and AI are enhancing our ability to preserve and celebrate traditional recipes while also pushing the boundaries of what is possible in the kitchen. This fusion of past and present is creating a dynamic culinary landscape that is both rooted in history and forward-thinking, offering endless opportunities for innovation and creativity.

Culinary traditions are a vital part of our cultural heritage, passed down through generations and preserved through family recipes and cooking techniques. These traditions reflect the history, values, and identity of a community, making them an essential aspect of cultural preservation. Modern technology is playing a crucial role in safeguarding these traditions, enabling us to document, share, and celebrate our culinary heritage in new and innovative ways.

Digital platforms and online communities are providing a space for individuals to share their culinary traditions with a global audience. By posting recipes, cooking videos, and cultural stories, people can connect with others who share their heritage and introduce their traditions to new audiences. This digital exchange of culinary knowledge is fostering a greater appreciation for the diversity of global cuisine and promoting cultural understanding and unity.

Robotics and AI are also helping to preserve traditional cooking techniques by offering precise control and consistency. For example, an AI-powered cooking system can replicate the exact steps and measurements required to prepare a traditional dish, ensuring that it is made correctly every time. This level of precision is particularly valuable for techniques that require a high degree of skill and expertise, such as artisanal bread baking or delicate pastry work. By preserving these techniques, we can ensure that traditional recipes are passed down accurately to future generations.

The fusion of culinary traditions and modern technology is also driving innovation in the kitchen. Chefs and home cooks are using technology to experiment with new ingredients, techniques, and presentation styles, creating dishes that blend the old and the new. This approach allows for a reinterpretation of traditional recipes, incorporating contemporary flavors and techniques while honoring their heritage. The result is a dynamic and evolving culinary landscape that celebrates both tradition and innovation, offering endless possibilities for creativity and exploration.

12

Chapter 12: Embracing the Social Kitchen of Tomorrow

As we look to the future, the social kitchen will continue to evolve, shaped by the ongoing interplay between culinary traditions and technological advancements. By embracing the possibilities offered by robotics and AI, we can create a kitchen that is more inclusive, sustainable, and connected. This vision of the social kitchen of tomorrow is one where food brings people together, fosters creativity, and enhances our quality of life. As we navigate this exciting journey, let us remember that at the heart of it all is the simple joy of sharing a meal with loved ones, creating memories that will last a lifetime.

The social kitchen of tomorrow will be a place where technology and tradition intersect, creating a seamless and harmonious cooking experience. Advanced appliances and robotic assistants will take on routine tasks, allowing cooks to focus on the creative and social aspects of meal preparation. Smart kitchen systems will provide personalized guidance and support, making it easier for individuals to maintain a healthy and enjoyable diet. These innovations will enhance convenience and efficiency, making cooking more accessible and enjoyable for everyone

13

Chapter 13: Culinary Traditions in the Digital Age

As we embrace the digital age, culinary traditions are finding new ways to thrive and evolve. Digital platforms and social media have become powerful tools for preserving and sharing traditional recipes, allowing people to connect with their cultural heritage and introduce it to a global audience. Online recipe databases, cooking blogs, and video tutorials provide a wealth of resources for anyone looking to explore and celebrate traditional cuisines. This digital transformation is ensuring that culinary traditions remain relevant and accessible in the modern world.

One of the key benefits of the digital age is the democratization of culinary knowledge. People from all walks of life can now access information and resources that were once limited to professional chefs and culinary experts. This accessibility is fostering a greater appreciation for diverse culinary traditions and encouraging individuals to experiment with new flavors and techniques. By sharing their culinary journeys online, people are building a sense of community and fostering cultural exchange.

The digital age is also promoting the preservation of endangered culinary traditions. As older generations pass down their recipes and techniques through digital platforms, they ensure that these valuable cultural treasures are not lost. This digital documentation is creating a lasting record of culinary heritage, preserving it for future generations. By leveraging the power of technology, we can celebrate and honor the rich diversity of global cuisine.

In addition to preserving traditions, the digital age is driving culinary innovation. Chefs and home cooks alike are using digital tools to experiment with new ingredients, techniques, and presentation styles. Online cooking challenges and competitions are inspiring creativity and pushing the boundaries of traditional cooking. This dynamic and evolving culinary landscape is a testament to the enduring power of food to bring people together and inspire innovation.

14

Chapter 14: The Role of Robotics in Professional Kitchens

Robotics is making a significant impact in professional kitchens, transforming the way restaurants and foodservice operations function. From automated cooking systems to robotic waitstaff, these technologies are enhancing efficiency, consistency, and safety in the culinary industry. By taking on repetitive and labor-intensive tasks, robotics allows chefs and kitchen staff to focus on more creative and value-added activities, improving the overall dining experience for customers.

Automated cooking systems, such as robotic fryers and grillers, ensure that dishes are prepared with precision and consistency every time. These systems can handle high-volume cooking, reducing the risk of human error and ensuring that each dish meets the same high standards. This level of consistency is particularly valuable in fast-paced restaurant environments, where maintaining quality and efficiency is essential.

Robotic waitstaff and service robots are also becoming more common in restaurants, enhancing the dining experience for customers. These robots can take orders, deliver food and drinks, and even interact with guests, providing a unique and engaging experience. By automating routine service tasks, restaurants can improve efficiency and provide a higher level of customer service. This integration of robotics into the front-of-house operations is

CHAPTER 14: THE ROLE OF ROBOTICS IN PROFESSIONAL KITCHENS

transforming the way restaurants operate, creating a more seamless and enjoyable dining experience.

The use of robotics in professional kitchens is also promoting safety and hygiene. Robots can handle hazardous tasks, such as working with hot surfaces and sharp tools, reducing the risk of injuries to kitchen staff. Automated cleaning systems ensure that kitchen surfaces and equipment are kept spotless, minimizing the risk of contamination and foodborne illnesses. These advancements are creating a safer and healthier working environment for culinary professionals.

15

Chapter 15: The Influence of Food Bloggers and Influencers

Food bloggers and influencers have become powerful voices in the culinary world, shaping trends and influencing the way people cook and eat. Through their online platforms, they share recipes, cooking tips, and food reviews, reaching a wide and diverse audience. These influencers have the ability to introduce new ingredients, techniques, and cuisines to their followers, inspiring them to explore and experiment in the kitchen. By leveraging their influence, they play a significant role in shaping modern culinary culture.

One of the key contributions of food bloggers and influencers is their ability to make cooking accessible and relatable. By sharing their personal experiences and culinary journeys, they demystify complex cooking techniques and inspire confidence in their followers. Their approachable and authentic content resonates with people, encouraging them to try new recipes and explore different cuisines. This accessibility is fostering a greater appreciation for the art of cooking and empowering individuals to take an active role in their culinary adventures.

Food bloggers and influencers also play a crucial role in promoting diversity and inclusivity in the culinary world. By showcasing a wide range of cuisines and cooking styles, they celebrate the rich tapestry of global culinary

CHAPTER 15: THE INFLUENCE OF FOOD BLOGGERS AND INFLUENCERS

traditions. Their platforms provide a space for underrepresented voices and cuisines to be heard and appreciated, promoting cultural exchange and understanding. This celebration of diversity is enriching the culinary landscape and encouraging people to embrace the flavors and traditions of different cultures.

The influence of food bloggers and influencers extends beyond their online platforms. Many collaborate with brands, restaurants, and culinary events, shaping industry trends and driving innovation. Their ability to connect with their audience and build a sense of community is a powerful tool for promoting new products, ingredients, and cooking techniques. By leveraging their influence, they are helping to shape the future of food and dining, creating a more vibrant and dynamic culinary world.

16

Chapter 16: The Future of Home Cooking with Robotics

The future of home cooking is being shaped by the integration of robotics and AI, creating a more convenient, efficient, and enjoyable cooking experience. From smart appliances to robotic kitchen assistants, these technologies are transforming the way we cook and interact with our kitchens. The smart home of the future will be equipped with advanced tools and systems that enhance the cooking process, making it more accessible and enjoyable for everyone.

Smart appliances, such as connected ovens, refrigerators, and dishwashers, are becoming increasingly common in modern kitchens. These devices can communicate with each other, providing a seamless and integrated cooking experience. For example, a smart refrigerator can suggest recipes based on the ingredients it has in stock, while a smart oven can adjust cooking times and temperatures to ensure perfect results. These innovations make cooking more convenient and efficient, allowing home cooks to focus on creativity and enjoyment.

Robotic kitchen assistants are also playing a significant role in the future of home cooking. These devices can perform a wide range of tasks, from chopping and mixing to cooking and cleaning. By taking on routine and labor-intensive tasks, robotic assistants free up time for home cooks to focus

CHAPTER 16: THE FUTURE OF HOME COOKING WITH ROBOTICS

on more enjoyable aspects of meal preparation. This increased efficiency and convenience make cooking more accessible to people of all skill levels, encouraging more individuals to explore their culinary passions.

AI-powered cooking systems are providing home cooks with expert guidance and support. These systems can offer personalized recipe recommendations, cooking tips, and troubleshooting advice, making it easier to achieve professional-quality results at home. By leveraging the power of AI, home cooks can expand their culinary repertoire and gain confidence in their cooking skills. This personalized guidance is fostering a greater appreciation for the art of cooking and inspiring a new generation of food enthusiasts.

17

Chapter 17: The Social Impact of Culinary Innovation

Culinary innovation is having a profound social impact, transforming the way we think about food and its role in our lives. From promoting sustainability to enhancing community engagement, these innovations are driving positive change and improving our quality of life. By embracing new technologies and approaches, we can create a more inclusive, sustainable, and connected food system that benefits individuals and communities alike.

One of the most significant social impacts of culinary innovation is the promotion of sustainability. Advances in food production, distribution, and preparation are helping to reduce waste, conserve resources, and minimize the environmental impact of our food choices. For example, urban farming and vertical agriculture are bringing food production closer to urban centers, reducing the carbon footprint associated with transportation. Sustainable cooking practices, such as zero-waste cooking and plant-based diets, are becoming more accessible and popular, contributing to a more eco-friendly food system.

Culinary innovation is also enhancing community engagement and social cohesion. Food has always been a powerful tool for bringing people together, and new technologies are amplifying this effect. Virtual cooking classes, online recipe sharing, and community food projects are creating opportunities for individuals to connect and collaborate, fostering a sense of belonging and unity. These initiatives are strengthening social bonds and promoting cultural exchange, enriching our communities and enhancing our quality of life.

In addition to promoting sustainability and community engagement, culinary innovation is driving economic growth and job creation. The development and adoption of new food technologies are creating opportunities for entrepreneurs, chefs, and foodservice professionals to innovate and grow their businesses. This economic impact is particularly significant in the context of the broader food system, where technological advancements are creating new markets and driving investment. By fostering innovation and supporting the growth of the culinary industry, we can create a more dynamic and resilient food economy.

The Social Kitchen: How Culinary Traditions and Robotics Shape Modern Communities

In "The Social Kitchen," explore the fascinating intersection of age-old culinary traditions and cutting-edge robotic technology. This book delves into how the kitchen, often the heart of a home, is evolving with the times. From the rich history of family recipes to the precision of AI-powered cooking systems, this book examines the ways in which food and technology are coming together to shape our modern communities.

Discover how culinary traditions define cultural identity and how technology is preserving and transforming these practices. Learn about the rise of smart kitchens and robotic assistants, making gourmet cooking accessible to everyone. Explore the social impact of culinary innovation, from promoting sustainability to enhancing community engagement.

"The Social Kitchen" is a journey through time, showcasing how food remains a powerful tool for connection and creativity. Whether you're a seasoned chef, a tech enthusiast, or someone who simply loves to cook, this book offers a unique perspective on the future of food and the kitchen's role in our lives. Join us in celebrating the fusion of tradition and innovation, and discover how the kitchens of tomorrow will continue to bring people together and enrich our communities.

www.ingramcontent.com/pod-product-compliance
Lightning Source LLC
LaVergne TN
LVHW010442070526
838199LV00066B/6142